Blastoff! Beginners are developed by literacy experts and educators to meet the needs of early readers. These engaging informational texts support young children as they begin reading about their world. Through simple language and high frequency words paired with crisp, colorful photos, Blastoff! Beginners launch young readers into the universe of independent reading.

Sight Words in This Book

a	eat	look
and	for	make
are	have	more
at	in	they
big	long	too

This edition first published in 2024 by Bellwether Media, Inc.

No part of this publication may be reproduced in whole or in part without written permission of the publisher. For information regarding permission, write to Bellwether Media, Inc., Attention: Permissions Department, 6012 Blue Circle Drive, Minnetonka, MN 55343.

Library of Congress Cataloging-in-Publication Data

Names: Rathburn, Betsy, author.
Title: Turkeys / by Betsy Rathburn.
Description: Minneapolis, MN : Bellwether Media, 2024. | Series: Blastoff! Beginners: Farm Animals | Includes bibliographical references and index. | Audience: Ages 4-7 | Audience: Grades K-1
Identifiers: LCCN 2023039757 (print) | LCCN 2023039758 (ebook) | ISBN 9798886877656 (library binding) | ISBN 9798886879537 (paperback) | ISBN 9798886878592 (ebook)
Subjects: LCSH: Turkeys--Juvenile literature. | Farm life--Juvenile literature.
Classification: LCC SF507 .R38 2024 (print) | LCC SF507 (ebook) | DDC 636.5/92--dc23/eng/20230831
LC record available at https://lccn.loc.gov/2023039757
LC ebook record available at https://lccn.loc.gov/2023039758

Text copyright © 2024 by Bellwether Media, Inc. BLASTOFF! BEGINNERS and associated logos are trademarks and/or registered trademarks of Bellwether Media, Inc.

Editor: Elizabeth Neuenfeldt   Designer: Laura Sowers

Printed in the United States of America, North Mankato, MN.

Table of Contents

Big Birds	4
What Are Turkeys?	6
Life on the Farm	14
Turkey Facts	22
Glossary	23
To Learn More	24
Index	24

Big Birds

Look at those turkeys.
They are big birds!

What Are Turkeys?

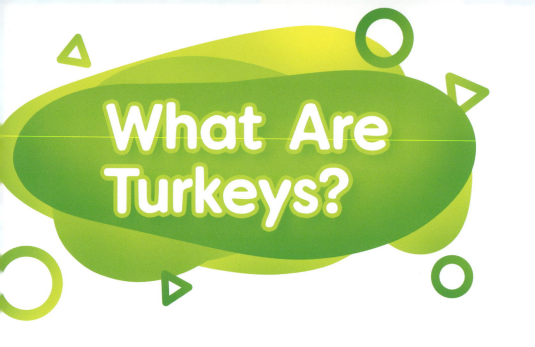

Turkeys are birds.
Males are toms.
Females are hens.

hens

They have long necks.
They have long legs.

They have **wattles**.
They have **snoods**.

They have **feathers**. Male tail feathers make a fan!

feathers

tail feathers

Life on the Farm

Turkeys stay in **pens**.

pen

They eat seeds. They eat plants and bugs, too!

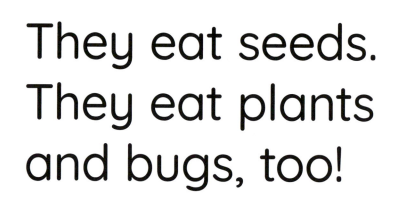

seeds

plants

bugs

Hens lay eggs.
Farmers care
for eggs.
Eggs make
more turkeys!

egg

Toms gobble
a lot.
They are loud!

Turkey Facts

Parts of a Turkey

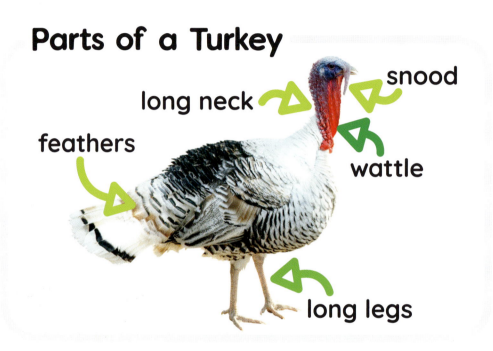

long neck

snood

feathers

wattle

long legs

Life on the Farm

stay in pens

eat

lay eggs

Glossary

feathers

soft coverings on turkeys

pens

closed places where turkeys live

snoods

pieces of skin that hang down the faces of turkeys

wattles

pieces of skin on the necks of turkeys

To Learn More

ON THE WEB

FACTSURFER

Factsurfer.com gives you a safe, fun way to find more information.

1. Go to www.factsurfer.com.

2. Enter "turkeys" into the search box and click 🔍.

3. Select your book cover to see a list of related content.

Index

birds, 4, 6
bugs, 16, 17
eat, 16
eggs, 18
farmers, 18
feathers, 12, 13
females, 6
gobble, 20

hens, 6, 18
legs, 8
males, 6, 12
necks, 8
pens, 14, 15
plants, 16, 17
seeds, 16
size, 4

snoods, 10, 11
tail, 12, 13
toms, 6, 7, 20
wattles, 10, 11

The images in this book are reproduced through the courtesy of: Eric Isselee, cover, p. 23 (feathers); Tsekhmister, p. 3; kaikups, pp. 4-5; bazilfoto, pp. 6, 7; Richard Wozniak, pp. 8-9; Casey Dugas, pp. 10-11; BalkansCat, p. 12; NARIN CHAIWORN, pp. 12-13; Jupiter Candy, pp. 14-15, 22 (stay in pens); Spalnic, p. 16 (seeds); Tim Graham/ Alamy, pp. 16-17; Michael G McKinne, p. 17 (plants); Davide Bonora, p. 17 (bugs); AnTish, p. 18; Natallia Ustsinava, pp. 18-19; Wirawan Sosuwansaman, pp. 20-21; siramatt1988, p. 22; ablokhin, p. 22 (eat); Nurlan Mammadzada, p. 22 (lay eggs); Quadxeon, p. 23 (pens); sergey kolesnikov, p. 23 (snoods); Gordana Sermek, p. 23 (wattles).